"If you think you're beaten, you are........"
- Walter D. Wintle

*"Don't pay the Ferryman,
'til he gets you to the other side........."*
- Chris de Burgh

Matters of the Heart

Robert Allen Eastwood

Photograph "Evening Sky at Renville" and Drawings
Michael J. Hurley

Cover Design
Proactive Design & Marketing

Additional Drawing
Gareth Kennedy

Introduction

Prior to his death, Bob left a wish list.

One of his wishes was that his poems, mostly penned while he was waiting for a heart transplant be published and the proceeds donated to Croí, the West of Ireland Cardiology Foundation.

Time has passed and this, at last, is the fulfillment of that wish.

Kathy Eastwood
November 2007

Dedications

I really should be dead. The fact that I am sitting here writing this instead, is a tribute to the love and prayers, skill and determination, support and compassion of so many people, that in truth, their name is legion.

The gift bestowed on me by my Donor's loved ones, is so great that my gratitude, wonder and thanks can never be adequately expressed.

My wife, Kathy, and my three children, Alan, Claire, and Brian were, and still are, a great source of strength. In many ways I had it easy, since if the going got too hard, I could always blank out, whereas they sat through it all. Even now I do not know how they did it.

The medical and support teams led by Maurice Nelligan in the Blackrock Clinic Dublin, by Kieran Daly at University College Hospital Galway, and John Hurley in the Mater Public Hospital in Dublin showed a level of professionalism and humanity for which I am eternally grateful and for which Ireland should be justly proud.

The level of support shown by the people of Oranmore and Maree to me, a "Blow In", was, and continues to be, wondrous. Thank you.

I could never name all the people involved in giving me a new life. I am sure that it will be understood if I make just one exception; my brother Edgar, whose encouragement was great, but who sadly died whilst visiting Galway in March 1998 and thus was unable to see the finished volume...

In The Beginning......

When you are dying, and you know that the only chance of life is a heart transplant, you have many thoughts and very many emotions. Initially you dwell upon the pain and the fear of the dying process, and all of us react differently according to our different philosophies and beliefs. After a while this recedes as death becomes your constant companion. You accept or reject, in much the same way as you would treat a distant relative whom you meet during a wedding party. You give them respect for who they are and their status, but otherwise you ignore them.

You begin to view death more in terms of that which you will no longer see or experience; a child's marriage; the dawning of the sun; the laughter in your lover's eyes. It is from these feelings that there is a great surge of reverence for life itself, which always brings you full circle, since your life depends on the death of another.

This is the brutal reality of the Heart Transplant's world. It will be a dreadful accident and the trauma of sudden death, which will give us life. Our thoughts constantly dwell upon the Donor. Will they come in time? What will be the nature of their death? What sort of person will they be? Will it be a man or a woman, married or single, father or brother?

These thoughts bring a great compassion for the loved ones of the Donor; for it is they who, in the midst of their own pain and torment, will be asked to think of the life and future of a stranger. These are the ones begged to consider, that from the ashes of their own tragedy, could spring the untold happiness of the recipient and his/her family.

Thus this small volume was born. It is an imperfect record of people and thoughts, situations and events that affected me during the year between having a triple by-pass, and the heart transplant. Some are funny, some sad. All of them, I hope, express my eternal gratitude to my Donor and those he/she left behind.

Robert Allen Eastwood
Oranmore, Co. Galway
August 2000

Contents

The Waiting

Tonight I lie awake again,
Waiting for the call,
Knowing that when, should it come,
Fear will finally strip herself for me.

Pain and I are like good friends,
Never far apart
And always thinking of each other,
Our bond is my surrendering, whimpering and tears.

Sadness is another matter,
As I dwell upon the things I may not see;
My children laughing, giggling, squabbling,
growing,
The un-ending love in those eyes of grey
I chose so long ago.

But what I'm really waiting for,
As deep within myself I peer,
Is for a simple man, a good or evil man,
A fit and healthy man,
To die.

The Hooded Man

I met a man today
In hooded cowl.
A man, so full of spite
And hate and anger,
That even the stars above
Could not light up
His countenance.

And when I met him,
He greeted me
With pain-wracked smile,
And sadness cupped my heart,
As, through my tears
I saw a face once remembered in my dreams,
Of long ago.

I met a man today,
So dressed in anguish and self doubt,
A despairing man
Whose love was dying in the wind
Of misplaced fury.
I met myself today-
And wept.

Silence

Silence is my succour.
She absorbs me
And gives me peace.
And when I feel like screaming at my destiny
She gathers me in her arms.

Silence is a place where evil goes to die;
Where dreams are built;
Where sunshine lifts a darkening soul;
Where futures stretch in all directions,
And paths of blue-bells promise much across each rise.

Silence lets me leave my pain behind.
She feeds me strength
And shows how things are meant to be.
She jests with me.
She cups my soul with laughter,
And gently walks me through the night.

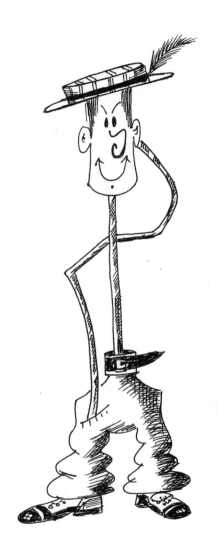

4

Ode To Fred

Fred was pencil thin;
Until you reached his middle,
And then he bulged!
But as my friend,
I'd never comment.

Firstly,
When drawn to his full height
He stood a good eight foot tall,
A Goliath to my six foot three;
And secondly,
He saved my life,
Not once, but many times.

He had another name of course,
Most technical,
And full of numbers;
But how could anyone attached to him
From dawn to dusk,
From week to week,
Sharing each, and every function,

Use such a label of a friend,
Who, even under most severe provocation,
Never broke wind from either end?

We would haunt
The endless corridors together,
His five toes splayed
On wheels so small and dainty
They would wwwhiissshhh along,
With not a squeak between them.

Then came the day
They said I did not need him any more!
I wept and begged,
Fred kept pumping,
But still the drip was disconnected.

At last I stood,
Unfettered,
Both my hands hanging free,
But all I heard was his bleeping,
As they wheeled him,
Away from me.

A Love Song

My love sits beside the birch tree,
And watches the waters lapping;
My love rides the moonbeams,
And holds the starlight in her hands;
My love rests in the meadow,
And weaves the primrose around her;
My love sings with the morning,
And lifts my heart with wonder;
My love is a willow tree,
And minds the bull-rushes;
My love is you,
And your smile,
My home-coming.

The Three Pebbles

Do you remember, love of mine,
How first we went
Hand in hand, along the shores,
Searching for we knew not what,
Yet knowing it was there for us?

Then finding it,
Cast high by tide and wind,
Perfectly shaped, and calling;
A wondrous pebble for our collection,
The one we had not started yet.

We took it home and cherished it,
But time is never idle,
And soon along some distant shores
We searched,
And much more quickly this time round
We found the perfect match,
And in our pleasure and our joy
We ceased to look for more.

And thus these two,
Both gleaming in their different ways,
Took up our lives,
As by the sea, hand in hand,
We did not trespass any more.

Then, Once along the mountain top you
stumbled,
I gripped you as you hit the ground,
But when you raised your eyes to mine,
So grey and full of love,
You showed me in your other hand
Why our pilgrimage was done.

And so we sit,
Still hand in hand,
And watch our trio grow,
As dimly in my memory
A voice sings,
Benedicamus Domino.

9

The White Buffalo

Fear came to me last night,
In another place.
She came, I think,
To show me that She could,
And let me feast upon her beauty.

Her eyes were the blue of a deep Norwegian fjord;
Her hair,
Long and blond.
She wore a skirt intricately patterned,
From a place and time I knew not.

She was tall,
A boyish figure,
And with slinking movements,
Thrusting out her hips,
She began to dance.
At last She stopped before me;
Her eyes were laughing,
And then She gave a girlish giggle
And my skin crawled
With this sound of crackling ice.

Slowly, her eyes bright with living fire,
She swept her hair across my face,
Eased up her skirts,
Revealing shapely, alabaster legs;
Then, one handed,
Teasingly,
She began to loosen her heavy blouse,
Not once taking her eyes from mine.

I am sweating now.
My chest,
A heavy weight, with darting pains,
The cramps beginning in my feet
And slowly knotting upwards.

She begins to sway;
I fight her with all my Faith,
Searching for the White Buffalo to rescue me.
She laughs,
And slowly drags her sharpened nails
Across my chest.

Suddenly, She is gone.
I am alone,
Bathed in torment, pain and sweat,
Shaking, like a rabbit,
Surviving, when the hawk has missed his dive.

I prayed then, as I had never prayed,
But no matter how I strained my ears,
I could not hear the drumming of the hoofs,
Of my White Buffalo.

Saint Paul

My beloved is sitting with me now,
As tiredness drips from her,
Like the melting hoar frost in the tundra,
When the sun breaks through.

My heart is bleeding for her,
And I find myself urging her to rest
Since whether I live or die lies with the Lord,
And shocked, I feel these words are true.

This year of pain and broken dreams,
I suddenly find
Has held more laughter, love and happiness,
Than most men see in all their lives.

A great contentment swells within me
As I dwell upon the future,
Knowing that when my time is up, I'll still fight,
And wondering whether that man from Tarsus
would understand.

grey

Was

On roo.. of cramped and grimy cottages,

Where rain and coal dust

Fought a war

As ancient as the ravaged hills,

Which wept,

As hills of slag buried grass,

And the scent of honeysuckle.

Then,

From the west another grey,

Of laughter, warmth and caring;

Sharing, gentle, strong, uplifting,

A merry grey;

That hid its pain and glowed with love

And steadfastness.

This grey I grew to love
And hold,
This grey of hope and fortitude,
This grey, so deep it had no end,
As in the eyes of you,
My love.

The Salt Cellar

Have you really ever wondered
How it feels deep down inside?
Pull it,
Push it.
Snatch it,
Grab it,
Throw it round the table.

I'm sure it must have feelings,
For once it did have social status,
And to sit,
Above it,
With it,
Below it,
Under it,
Really meant where you were
In the general worldly order.

No wonder it now stands defiant,
In alliance with the pepper.
Just to stand and pass no comment,
Just to give what is demanded,
Contained within a compound plastic,
Refraining from a word or comment;
Lonely, haughty, with disdain,
Feeling useful, but unwanted,
Knowing its time would come again.

The Cloister

The gate ajar was beckoning,
So he passed through,
A pilgrim in a land
Of cabbages and small fruit trees,
Neat turf,
Potatoes in their graves being born.

At first a silence, pressing, clinging,
Hemmed in by walls of stone.
But then a jingling, giggling, laughing,
Tumbling, juggling, bounding,
Giddy, swirling, smiling,
Throng of children
Came and danced with him.

In this sunlight paradise
Of peace and playfulness,
He met and romped and laughed
With children not yet born;
Who could not, would not, ever be,
Whose birth in dreams and self denial
Chained them everlastingly
Within this cloister of silent prayer.

He journeyed on with heavy heart
To within the house,
Drawn by hope and lilting anthems,
Songs of joy, of love, of peace,
As through the heavy grill he peered
Locked and bolted from within,
Scorning parents, brothers, sisters,
Loving none, thus loving all.

Yet all he saw were fathers weeping
For daughters lost;
Enclosed and chaste,
Matins and vespers
Being their chance to catch a glimpse
Of a child, still loved and wanted,
But spurning all the old embraces.

Thus the pilgrim
Heavy with the thought of loss and pain,
Reached the outside gates of this enclosure,
Still searching,
But with down cast eyes,
And did not see,
Nor did not hear,
The tree tops whisper.....
"Suffer these children to come unto me,
For theirs is the Kingdom ...."

The Sparrow

And as the Sparrow
With broken wing
Fell dying to the ground,
She found the hand of God,
And took me there.

False Conceptions

She came to me today,
The hard one.
She had her troubles,
Which, by all that she held dear,
Were great;
The tear I spied was slowly
Creeping down her cheek,
But before its tale was told,
Was brushed away and hidden.

She came to me today,
The hard one;
She spoke of how her heart,
So oft impregnable,
Had been breached and sacked,
Raped, with no intent of kindness,
By the one to whom she'd
Opened up its doors.

She came to me today,
The hard one;
And spoke of things,
I'd thought that she'd not know.
She's sighing now and sadness,
With it's wistful gaze
Has settled on her furrowed brow.

She came to me today,
The one I'd mocked as stone;
And for a while,
I thought myself a fool,
For which of us can truly see,
The depths of other's feelings,
As we search the window's of their souls?

Grey-Eyes' Friend

Long, long legs,
Beneath a skirt of slits,
Which flash and disappear
And then go on forever.

Her ankles are well turned,
As Lermontov must have dreamed,
In Saint Petersburg,
Before
The Revolution.

She is my Grey-Eye's friend,
This witch-doctor
To my soul,
Who has, so many times,
Saved a mind from its insanity.

Today we celebrate
The positioning of the spheres,
Which did predict our meeting
So many years ago,
As all the old gods laughed,
And summoned us to Erin.

The Screaming City

This Hybrid,
This quite literally New Man,
Who once was haunted by his mistress, Pain,
Can now clearly hear
The thundering hoofs of the White Buffalo.

But he's hearing other things;
Things he had long forgotten
In the nightmares of his other life
Before he had ever heard of Erin,
Or seen the pier at Annaghdown.

He hears a city screaming;
A common thing where he was born,
As wailing sirens
Drown laughter and the barking dogs,
And silent weeping stills the child.

The Cordless Telephone

This cordless telephone,
Which I must carry like an Albatross,
Is dull grey,
Bar it's red eye,
Which glares at me,
Resentfully.

It must be clutched like a leprous stump,
For my Beloved checks on me,
Many, many times a day;
To see that I am well
And share her love for me.

Each time I hear it pulsing,
I hesitate to switch it on,
Fearing to hear the news,
That my heart has come;
To know that it is time
For me to enter the arena,
Give Caesar my salute,
And so begin my dance with Death.

To be assured that,
With one small slip upon the sand
I will be lost,
Carried to the banks
Of the dark and dismal Styx
And forced, despite my tears and screaming
torment
To give the ferryman all my silver,
And cross, to waiting Agamemnon.

My telephone is cordless,
And she is carried like a suckling babe;
She comforts me like little else,
For she is my contact
With the world beyond my doors,
Should I need assistance,
Or a pint of milk.

It will be her
Whose gentle tones will summon me
For my new heart;
Permitting me to slip
Beneath the waters of the Jordan,
And have the Baptist raise me up,
Reborn.

If it is written,
Then once again I will be free
To take the hand of she who loves me,
And walk outside these walls
Which have become my world;
To taste the sea upon the wind
And feel the sun across my back,
Praising God for each new day
And all their endless opportunities.

Pilgrim

I gazed into the father's eyes,
And watched the tears
Being born,
As pain squeezed them from his heart.

The mother, head bowed,
Sobbed gently,
As if afraid that she would wake him,
Whilst she stroked his now dry hair.

Sweet Pilgrim!
What made you stumble
And drop your gaze from the Grail,
We all are cursed and blessed to seek?

Did you forget the Herons across the bay,
The sun dancing on the Corrib,
The humming of the bees at Barna Woods,
The boats anchored down in Renville?

Or was it that,
When the blackness gripped your soul,
You were so tired,
The road so hard and long,
You felt it time to lie and rest?

Brother

My brother's brother called today,
With salutations,
In facsimile of the perfect toast,
Wishing me good health and happiness.

He was the greatest and the sweetest of us all;
The only one in the crucible of the smelter
Who could make the Sweeper smile,
And the Master talk of cabbages and kings.

He was the father I found but twice in all my life;
As a crumpled rag with coal gas skulking,
In a neglected plot, as his wife would wish
In punishment.

He chased me with the skin of a dead snake,
Shed tears when I was dragged, drowning,
From the local pond,
And clapped, when I spoke
Of chasing the setting sun to Erin.

Now he is dying.
As he raises up his glass in mock salute
I curse him for the pain he causes,
Spending, apparently without remorse,
The love I've hoarded for us both.

The Man Who Loved Lighthouses

Small.
A shock.
The type of shock Yevtoshenko
Must have felt,
The last and first time
He saw Hemmingway.

His voice,
Gentle, teasing, leading, teaching,
Spreading advice, so disguised,
One never saw the gift,
And so was spared
The anger of acceptance.

From him I learned of lighthouses;
Their history;
Their place within the hearts of men,
And saw him drift away,
When he sensed a loss of hope
Upon the breeze.

At such times,
Would he know
That he himself had been transformed?
And his beacon,
Held aloft by conviction,
And fuelled by his integrity,
Was the only lighthouse we would trust?

The Piece of Toast

The piece of toast lay on the plate;
White bread grilled to a golden hue
And covered with butter from the fridge-
Its smell arousing me with lust.

I knew I couldn't eat it.
They said, "Yes Sir, we did a Thingee,
And it is a pity it's not working very well-
But not to worry,
Our transplant figures are really very good!"

The consultant and his team excelled,
Amidst the tests and taking blood,
They'd crack the greatest jokes,
And in their caring and their sharing
All they wanted were all my teeth.

Now being but a simple chap
I thought this fair,
I would give a man my teeth,
And I would get his heart,
The ultimate in the verb "To Barter"

So toothless I became.

Everyone said, "You're looking good!"

And I would boast about the strength of weetabix

In warm milk - many times a day.

But when I saw the piece of toast;

The butter melting, the scent arousing,

I lost control and seized it,

Sinking my gums right through the crispy crust

To its warm and soft sweet centre.

As I munched and crunched, instead of slurping,

I suddenly thought about the fairness of my deal;

The barter of my teeth for someone else's heart;

And may God forgive me,

I was glad.

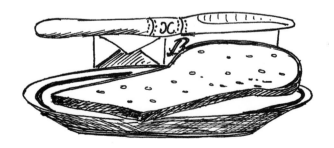

50 Years On

He paused and looked at her,
She smiled,
He thought a little wistfully,
But then, perhaps she did have cause.

A little slowly, he lowered himself,
And coughed self consciously.
"I came," he said, "I kept the date."
Her smile continued.

Like friends all do,
He asked," You remember....?
Of course you do......"
As far behind the music flared.

"I tried to make you see..."
His fingers twisted in a knot,
The knuckles creaking
With the unaccustomed shape.

"Oh Dearest,
I tried to make you understand
How things had changed
But had not altered."

She was still the same, he thought,
Brocaded blouse warmly hugging
The still full-shaped
And well formed breasts.

Around him, he felt a stir.
The music changed, he didn't notice.
He glanced across the gap and saw
The group approaching.

He stooped and swiftly brushed his lips
Across the powdered cheek.
Her scent had changed..
He grinned. "I noticed," he whispered softly.

The priest,
With puzzled frown,
Edged forward, hesitantly.
The incense swung slowly from the silvered chain.

"Good-Bye, my sweet, I really tried."
At last he turned to go.
He shuffled slowly across the flags
And out the heavily wooded doors.

Behind him, the organ roared;
Bach! She would have liked that he mused.
A tear crept across the wrinkled face,
"Dear God, accept this soul," he prayed.

Choices

I stood beside the dry stone wall,
Gazed across the waters,
Felt the heat of long lost summers
And drank the air that did not breathe.

Across the bay, scattered,
Like the toys of some disgruntled child
Lay the boats that were not there,
Excepting, from a thousand hallyards
Came the strummings of ten thousand
harpstrings.

Then I realized that all the boats were choices,
Some I'd seized and some I hadn't,
That in the end it did not matter
For fate herself had brought us here.

It came to me that my free will
Upon which I'd lavished so much suffering,
Groping for the choice to change the future,
Was but a dream,
And reality
Was the singing from those distant spars…

Bird Song

The birds are singing now.
My opening eyes see just a tip of sun,
And a host of wheeling, darting figures,
Whose songs are overlaid and interwoven
Like the richest Berber's carpet.

"Which type?" I hear you ask.
I laugh.
"A Cormorant or Swallow,
Racing Bluetit or pink blushed Flamingo,
Arrogant Peregrine, or disgruntled Crow,
A lonely Blackbird, or pristine Dove ?"

Where I come from,
Across the cut out near the gasworks,
We only knew of two;
The pigeon and the sparrow,
Both foragers like me.

I love it though,
As from my bed, across the bay,
The hills of Clare do beckon me,
And this song ,
This richness sent by God,
Does somehow comfort me.

Unidentified

She paused,
As if alone and wondering.
The rain was light
And held her hair in droplets;
Bedecking her
With shimmering jewels of gold.

Across the gravelled pathways,
Trim with caring,
I followed her,
Until I saw them - sheltering.

They beckoned me,
As a friend,
Pleading for recognition,
Lying together in rows,
Without adornment.

Tenderly I spoke with them;
I watched their rest,
Their uniformity
And was held with so much emptiness.

The rain was heavy now,
Thickening,
Clouding everything,
The other stones felt closer,
As if, in understanding,
They should comfort me.

She startled me with a hand,
A loving smile.
"Tomorrow is our Wedding Day.
We must return."
I wondered where.

Humbly
I took the small gloved hand
And headed for the gates.

Just for a moment
I felt them call me back,
Those grey stone slabs,
The few who'd come to Erin's Isle to sleep.
No names,
No monuments,
Save some few letters,
Unidentified.

The Bath-Tub

Cast iron,
With four carved feet
To hold her firm,
A glorious relic from the fifties
Or beyond.

She had such status
When first erected,
That she was given a mighty room,
At whose centre she awaits,
Like Victoria, not amused.

My white angels
Bring me to her,
For absolution,
Or ablutions,
I'm never certain which.

Yet as their fingers
Flutter over me,
Kneading, stroking, scrubbing, scratching,
The water hot,
The soap-suds lapping,
I sense that I'm in heaven,
And everything is well.

Glastonbury

A grove of green mossed trees
Attracted me;
Dappled light, with foxgloves dancing;
A moon of stones
Fresh washed with rain drops;
Crowns of Mistletoe
With silver birch in waiting.

Stooping slightly,
I entered in
A grove of stillness, quietness and peace.

A slim figure
With battered hose and doublet frayed,
Stood and gazed at me;
An ageless face,
So young,
I felt a thousand, thousand years had welcomed him.

"What is this place?" He asked
"Glastonbury"

He smiled at that, as if He heard
Ten thousand voices echo out the name
In doubt,
In wonder, so few with hope,
And less, with certainty.
"Who are you?"
"I am my uncle's nephew"
"And his business?"
"Tin, from your mines"
A Cornish jest with no-one laughing

"And your father?"
"His business......"
Such a pause,
As time grew old and young in waiting.
"You", He sighed.

"And yours?" I asked, confused.
This time he smiled,
With warmth and joy
"Some say 'tis carpentry,
But I am here
For all those lost in Purgatory".

Then the dream was gone,
As in your eyes I looked,
And saw not brown, but steely blue,
A skin not darkly tanned, but pink;
And to you and Him I share
My heartfelt thanks,
My love,
As was not done
In Glastonbury.

Double Bed a Shilling

An affable man is he;
His locks tight curled in grey.
Much humour has he gathered,
Of the most dry variety,
Which he spends without a thought,
And so disguised
'Tis often missed by careless ear.

He has his views -
Carved from life's experience;
A man must provide at any cost;
Once through his door he's king,
His castle is inviolate;
Generosity is the bye-word,
And taking is a mortal sin.

But these ruled which he applies to others,
To himself he is equally as strict,
So I raise my glass
To a friend of the four Farrellys,
And know my life is richer
For hearing Percy French.

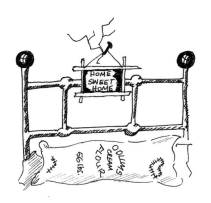

Whisperings

The Pilgrim paused,
As he heard his New Year's Gift
Whisper, across the years;
Gently stroking dreams,
And stirring memories he had so long forgot.

From her he'd learned so much;
Had seen the bluebells
Dance beneath the trees on College Hill;
Caused eyes to sparkle with delight,
As a Saxon mouth
Mispronounced the Old One's tongue;
Was comforted,
The day that Masefield died;
And wept,
Over desolate Sengennedd.

Only now,
In another land
Where Troubadours and Bards
Still weave their Druid magic,
Does he begin to understand
The words of Robert Frost.

Recovery Road

The transplant road is hard,
Even if you have the Faith,
And get the visits
That will break your heart
With their love,
Since, when all is quiet,
Doubt will come and sit with you.

The little angels flutter,
With impish grins,
And crisp white uniforms,
With gentle, lilting tones,
Eyes sparkling,
As they dare you to concede defeat,
On this, their shift.

Instead you reach for virgin paper,
And try to codify these thoughts,
To formulate a purpose;
To re-establish any reason
To face your body's next assaulting,
For your drip is tissuing out,
Again.

Altered

The name's the same
Though little else
For the man whose heart stopped beating
During Pentecost.

A reader who no longer reads,
His books untouched and gathering dust,
Instead, at peace with scented woods,
Set squares, gimlets and odd shaped saws.

And then this man, this other man,
This man whose heart was changed,
Looks in those eyes so grey,
Feels the love and knows
He would not wish to be another.

Resurrection

Yesterday,
I began a trip
I know not where,
From a place I was not sure.

Today,
I met my love
Whom I'd forgotten,
As she led me from the darkness.

Tomorrow,
I will clasp your hand,
As we again
Explore the joys of life together.

A Woman's Lot

Our Pilgrim lay as his Master had,
So many centuries before,
With a cloth,
Loosely across his loins,
And a scar, so deep, cut in his frame.

And in this modern crypt
Of drips and respirators, instead of stone,
Again a woman sits, head bowed,
As women have these ages passed,
Beside their men, rocking with their prayers.

His soul was in another place;
A lush green valley
Besides clear, sweet, still waters,
Listening for a call to go or stay,
Uncertain from whom or why.

But in this world of blood and tears,
Where ecstasy and pain are oft entwined,
His lover, wife, companion, friend,
Felt each dart of pain and ragged breath,
And relived each torment a thousand, thousand times.

Much later,
Whilst on a grassy knoll,
The sun loitering across the heavens,
He pondered on the pain and suffering,
The waiting, pleading, praying, begging,
That women endure so willingly,
And men can barely comprehend.

Merlin Park

I saw no Etna smoking,
Nor snake
Drinking at my water trough
As Lawrence did,
But broad, rich swards
Of undulating grasslands,
Gently rolling,
In this western light.

There are no poppies
As seem to crowd out Monet's fields,
But buttercups and Daises,
Thrusting gaily, proudly,
Up towards a cobalt heaven,
And scattered trees,
Whose greens and copper browns
Cascade against the senses,
As waves upon the land.

Still.
Then darting, diving, listening, turning,
Stopping, starting, nibbling, scratching;
Silently scampering,
Gleefully dancing,
A group of rabbits burst into view,
And with such joy and jollity in their ranks,
My heart was lifted,
And the pain within my soul,
Was lessened.

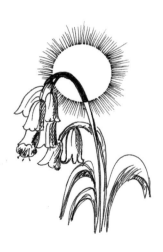

The Wonderful Gift

Pain and subdued lighting
Always seem in partnership
When time is cold
Before first light.

He'd found many things were loathsome,
But the melding of commode
With stomach cramps
Before a group of crisp white uniforms,
Held its own indignity.

Yet strangely,
On a night as pain had tugged
And sweat had dripped,
When his own rank odour
Fought to overwhelm him,
His only thought
Was of a hand outstretched,
Bringing him a sun kissed daffodil.

On The Pier at Oranmore

Sun-kissed, the bollard beckoned me,
Along the pier
From out the shadow of the castle,
And begged me sit.

We waited,
As many such had done in ages past,
Suspecting, but not certain,
That soon a guest would come.

I felt a gentle breeze,
As in the distance, out passed the point,
A dot emerged,
Growing with the keening of a single gull.

The curragh's prow was high, and painted black,
But still I waited,
Until the Ferryman shipped his oars,
And looked at me with hand outstretched.

But with a heart that was not mine,
Donated out of pain and suffering,
I wept for all the love and prayers,
Oran had sacrificed for me.

At last I shook my head,
And turned my gaze unto the sun;
Listened to the creaking rowlocks,
And savoured this new life beating through me.

73

Four Weeks

Four weeks ago,
I was a dead man walking,
Now I am a live man crawling.
Still they ask me how I feel?

Should I tell them of the pain,
From my torn fingernail?

Metanoia

A swirling, curling, clinging mist,
A whiteness
Blemishing the hilltops,
Long abandoned by the warmth of laughter.

The willow wept,
Its silent screams,
So highly tuned
Only a soul could hear.

The goshawk screeched,
Its wings outspread,
Motionless,
Above a figure
Fresh sprung upon my hillside.

He's closing now,
With droplets
Hanging from his cowl,
Like promises of joy or pain.

This time,
With straightened back
And beating heart
I meet him,
In a silence filled with crashing thunder.

The hooded cowl
Is lifted,
Showing scars of bitterness and loss,
But healing now,
And in those eyes
A different look,
Forgiveness